Where Memory Gathers

Fr. Ed

3-11-12

Where Memory Gathers

Baseball and Poetry

Edward R. Ward

Forum Press
San Francisco

Copyright © Edward R. Ward

Forum Press is an imprint of Rudi Publishing

Rudi Publishing, 12 Geary St., Suite 508, San Francisco CA 94108

Printed in the United States of America

ISBN 0-945213-33-6

Cover illustration, *Cobb Stealing Third*, by Mike Schacht (with permission).

"Baseball and the Law" has appeared in *Baseball Research Journal*, vol. 25 (1996).
"A Fevered Time" has appeared in *The Carmelite Review*, vol. 36, no. 5 (May 1, 1997).

Library of Congress Cataloging-in-Publication Data

Ward, Edward R.,
Where memory gathers : baseball and poetry / Edward R. Ward
p.   cm.
Includes bibliographical references.
ISBN 0-945213-33-6
1. Baseball—Poetry.   I. Title.
PS3573.A7313W47 1998
811'.54—dc21   98-7433
CIP

Contents

Introduction   vii

I. Spaces/Places
    Baseball in the Rockies   3
    Baseball in Indianapolis   4
    The Black Game   6
    Acrostic, 1958   8
    Louisville   9
    The Dixie Game   10
    Brooklyn Bridegrooms, 1890   12
    The Newark Game   14
    Baseball in Syracuse   15
    Baseball @ SoHo, nyc   16
    Columbus: Summer Game   17
    Baseball Along the Genesee   18
    Nowhere But Peoria   19
    Minor Baseball   20
    Home   22

II. Some Active Reconstruction
    Memory   25
    At Ten   26
    July's Game   27
    Chronology   28
    Around the Horn   29
    Gone But Not . . .   30
    A Special Care   31
    A Fevered Time   32
    Second   34
    Aches and Pains   35

Safe?   36

Down in the Count   37

1890/one eight nine zero   38

Scores and Tallies   40

Landscape: Baseball   41

Babe Ruth, Our Hero   42

Artificial Class   44

Seven Year Old's Dream   45

Baseball, 1845-   46

Some Musings on Ice   48

Nostalgia   50

III. Indoor Games

Definition   53

One Revocable License, Please   54

Warning   56

Theories, Very Possible 38   57

Religion and the Game   58

The Game and Time   60

Riddle   62

The Chart   63

Music and the Game   64

Limited Power   65

Ordeal   66

Manager's Guide   67

Numbers and the Game   68

Baseball and the Law   70

Food and the Game   72

Villanelle   73

The Corporate Game   74

B4Real   76

Anagram   77

Additional Reading   79

Introduction

How does one write a beginning to a book of poetry that takes on two subjects as disparate as poetry and baseball?

Babe Ruth was said to enjoy a cold beer, not verses by T. S. Eliot, who was seven years Ruth's senior. Hank Aaron and Eddie Mathews were teammates on the field, but off the field the two didn't go to the nearest poetry reading. There's still no such thing as "Poetry Night" at the ballpark. Maybe there will be sometime, somewhere, though.

How does one put poetry ("exact words in perfect order") and baseball ("two teams of nine") together? One does so slowly and, I am convinced, with much pleasure.

Poetry and baseball do share some common ground.

First, says Roland Garrett, baseball "offers enormous scope to the imagination." A lazy fly ball to center, a perspiring pitcher, and a close play at third can parallel the life experiences of many fans in the stands. In a more poetic vein, Christopher Collins writes that the poet's imagination gives a name to what is seen, and the naming becomes a revelation to those who read what has been put to paper. The drama of seeing the pitcher standing tall on the mound and dominating those at bat is something many of us would like to do from time to time. The mix of the game, the imagination, and the printed page seems easy. Robert Francis sees a different world in which the pitcher exists, since he writes, "The others throw to be comprehended. He throws to be a moment misunderstood."

Second, Donald Hall speaks of "the momentary grace of order" found in the game of baseball, and it seems that little explanation is needed about how the game's plays take place in an ordered and intelligible way. Batting out of order is a violation of the rules. Balking on the part of the pitcher is forbidden, too. Christopher Merrill parallels baseball's sense of order by saying, "Language is an order larger than any individual; poets surrender to that order, hoping to discover in the process meanings they were not aware of when they sat down to write." John Ciardi warns us that the language of classification should not overpower the language of experience. He was speaking of poetry and the lives reflected in it; he might have been thinking of baseball, too.

Third, baseball is American. So were Walt Whitman and Marianne Moore, both of whom knew their baseball. Robert Frost once said, "Poets are like baseball pitchers. Both have their moments. The intervals are the tough things."

Fourth, moments of significance and the intervals between them are a delight to ponder both in the context of clock-less baseball and time-less poetry. Innings completed (despite errors) and stanzas finished (despite erasures) offer the opportunity to think of what has been and what is, what might be, and what should have been. Memory and imagining find a home in baseball and poetry. The "successive instants" we humans have on this earth will be well spent with both notepad and nine innings yet to be enjoyed.

Fifth, baseball and poetry are closely connected to memory, myth, and metaphor. Volumes have been written about those three "m" words. We are indebted to Donald Hall for his gem, "Baseball . . . is a place where memory gathers."

Sixth, baseball and poetry ("chosen sounds," we are told) both contain much beauty. A double play that takes a team out of trouble in the ninth inning can be a thing of beauty, both for the pitcher on the field as well as for the fan trained in observing ballet from the stands. Carl Sandburg's "Chicago" is beautiful, too, both for the English major and for the season ticket holder who is not an English major.

Seventh, baseball and poetry can be both simple and complex. Baseball Hall of Fame announcer Jack Brickhouse has said on several occasions, "A man either gets to first base or he doesn't; he either scores or he doesn't; the team with the most scores wins." On the other hand, comedian Bob Newhart did a skit years ago involving a phone conversation with baseball's Abner Doubleday. Upon being told some of the rules of baseball, Newhart remarks to Doubleday, "This is the most complicated game I have ever heard of." Poetry is also in this double bind. Whitman's "So Long!" seems pretty easy, but at the same time may not be so simple. The same goes for John Vance Cheney's "San Francisco."

Eighth, baseball and poetry offer a brief glimpse of what life really and truly should be about. Life is striving, winning, losing, and surviving. Some might recall that historian Perry Miller has written about how Americans should work at achieving, not inheriting. One can achieve in both baseball and poetry. Read "Night Game" by Rolfe Humphries for more proof.

Ninth, both baseball and poetry show the fallibility of human life. Getting at least one more swing after fouling off a 3–2 pitch shows that there is still some hope after all. Those who write know that pencils are still made with erasers on one end. Those erasers point to the writer's heart.

Of course, many other connections involving baseball and poetry and their interdependence could be explored. The two involve an interplay between past and present, says James Olney. Mary Oliver speaks of poetry's blend of heart and mind. So does baseball. How the two topics allow us to re-fashion and re-imagine the world might also be examined.

This book is written for those who may not know an aubade from a sacrifice bunt. Awareness can be increased, however, by taking a pad of paper and a pencil to a game. Watch what happens when a warm sun, a cold soft drink, no clock, and a few close plays at home come together. Let the mind and the heart wander. The knowledge of sestets will come later.

Some will notice several references to geography in my poems. This is in part because I believe that baseball is best understood and best enjoyed when viewed "in place." I do not recommend trying to appreciate the game by watching television. To get the real flavor of baseball in Indianapolis one is well advised to go there with notepad in hand, of course. Voices using a "vulgar" tongue must be heard. This is true of baseball as it is played in the Lehigh Valley in baseball-rich Pennsylvania, and in Rockford, Illinois, too.

I am indebted to others who have written skillfully about baseball. Writers like Richard Crepeau and Steven A. Riess come to mind, as do Donald Honig, John Holway, and George Will. I am also indebted to people like Lewis Turco. He has spent hours (many innings?) trying to show us a few things about the English language when used in poetry.

I make no excuses or alibis for my use of the English language, by the way. I love and enjoy English. It's an important language, in no small part due to its ability to reach so many people. Bill Bryson's statement about English being one of the world's great growth industries gets my attention, too.

Please don't look for a social function in my poetry. No lofty social purpose is being suggested or recommended.

The works listed in "Additional Reading" may spur readers to give baseball ("the national pastime") and poetry ("horizontal lines") a try. My attempts herein offer an invitation for others to walk the same path bringing two things of beauty a little closer.

Finally, Tess Gallagher may put things in the best perspective when she writes, "With all the modern time-savers, we have no better machine for the reinvention of time than the poem. I would not trade my least-loved poem for a Polaroid snapshot. The real time-savers are those that accommodate the mind, the heart, and the spirit at once." She is right.

And I myself might add, "Play ball!"

Edward R. Ward

I.

Spaces
and Places

Baseball in the Rockies

Winds, active still, descend and ascend.
Peaks rise.

"High altitude, low multitudes," we're told.

Pioneers all, and "a precious dust" draws folks.
Open spaces do, too, on water-wanting soil.

Jobs, on twin ribbons, appeal.
"Foreigners" an ordeal.

Call the roll:

Billings	Cheyenne
Leadville (Blues!)	Ogden
Pueblo	Colorado Springs
Missoula	Great Falls
Longmont (Utes!)	Helena
Butte (Copper Kings!)	

Denver plays major role in first year: 4,483,270 fan(atic)s.

Play the game:

a ball of 5 ounces
9 frames (at least)
2 teams (at most)
no boredom (at all)

Watch curves and altitude. Benders bend 25% less!

Welcome!

3

Baseball in Indianapolis

Car-crazy fans and basketball nuts meet: a pleasant mania.

First-look bland folks deceive: farm,
factory, and
grits meet. They agree on baseball.

Indianapolis
Blues
Hoosiers
ABC's
Clowns
Indians

Minor Wilson "Mickey" Heath,
Clyde Kluttz,
Gary Peters, and
Razor Shines: 4 stars at Bush (not Busch).

Rain delay? Time to savor 1914 club: 88-65.

Perfect game? 7/4 at 74 degrees. No put-outs 7 to 4.
Take 74 to get there.

Triple pleasure: vines at Bush (1931-1995),
a blast over lights in left, and
post-game dreaming.

Majors arrive in extra innings?
Cost runs thru sign at third.
Narrow lines compete with large dreams at 46225.

Stranded at third: feeble Tribe bats amid hostile arms.

Batter up!

The Black Game

Call the roll:

Crutchfield, Jimmie
Finch, Rayford
Forrest, Percy
Gibson, Josh
Green, Pumpsie
Manley, Effa
Turner, Etwood

Numbers tell: Roy Dandridge (MVP American Association 1950).
Record books swell: Monte Irvin (.458 NYG World Series 1951).

Nines merit naming:

Chicago American Giants
Jacksonville Red Caps
Newark Eagles
Kansas City Monarchs
Pittsburgh Crawfords
Cleveland Buckeyes

Crowd (51,723) arrives "two to a mule" for Chicago game, 1943.

Bathrooms?	Separate
Home to second?	Equal
Dollars?	Unequal
Skills?	Solid, not three-fifths!

Names attract: Doby, Mays, Aaron, Bonds.
Racism detracts: supper on the curb, breakfast on the run.

These a fact:
talent abundant; accomplishments, too.

Acrostic, 1958

E nergetically we ran
B elieving in the game.
B aseball
E xited, however.
T otally, abruptly, and
S adly.

Louisville

batter up. no bluegrass here. many patrons
attend. a gentle breeze, too. dial 1-800-slugger.
remember the birds, not the horses. a julep
lasts. stars include "Pudgie" Delehanty (1909),
Grover Cleveland Lowdermilk (1913). here small
beats large. dixie talk, southern walk despite
Rule 1.04: "home northeast." indy and buff no
heed. nashville? sing alone. columbus? good-bye.
hello to you all.

The Dixie Game

Warm days and better nights stay.
The game lives well below the 37th.

Macon shines.
Engel, Chattanooga, too.
Rickwood, Birmingham as well.
Sulphur Dell, Nashville, also.

The roll is long: Little Rock
                    Durham
                    Asheville
                    Charleston
                    Nawlins
                    Memphis
                    Atlanta
                    Richmond.

"Whites only" and "Colored" play.
Race abides "root and branch."

A sense of defeat endures.

Black Barons and Grays walk to the side.
Behavior uncivil.

Some arrive "two to a mule."
Others recall "forty acres and a mule."

The game at times sadder. But lasts. And lasts.
Stars galore, however:
George Christopher "Hickory" Jackson
at Shreveport,
John William Joseph "Bunny" Roser
at Norfolk,
William Beattie Feathers
at Knoxville.

New days give way to new ways.

Brooklyn Bridegrooms, 1890

Grooms glow in second-Harrison time:

            884 runs scored

            3.05 ERA

            349 bases stolen

Stars shine in "base ball" galaxy:

            "Oyster" Burns

            Adonis Terry

            Germany Smith

            Darby O'Brien

Fanatics, called "kranks" once, watch closely:

1 sub per game

0 clocks

2 umps

7 thinning stretch

9 frames

0 worry

            10-27-90: Game Six of Series vs. Louisville

What a team these Grooms,
       but quiet time looms (18 years until Ebbets).

until

    until

       until . . .

            Time does not wait.

"Wait till next year!!!"

No sadness till '93 death of Darby, cf
No mention of (trolley) Dodgers till '99

Thank you, Grooms!

The Newark Game

Passaic waters (1) move, if slowly.
New York breezes come, if briefly.

Jersey "base ball" (born 1855) awaits.

Sun-filled names are bright:
    Monte Irvin
    Joseph Michael "Double" Dwyer
    Mule Suttles
    Vic Raschi

History is right: Ruppert Stadium (born "Davids" 1926).

Names are bright:
    Eagles
    Bears

Burden not light:
jobs wanting at Broad and Market.

facts: 1937 awesome
fax: 201-491-BEAR   (2)
email: fans@newarknjball   (3)

The sun struggles; so does life today.

---

(1) See William Carlos Williams
(2) fictitious
(3) ditto

14

Baseball in Syracuse

City charter arrives 1847.

Cool winds visit as roll is called:
Newell Park
Star Park
Athletic Field
Hallock Park
Archbold Stadium
Star Park II
MacArthur Stadium (1934–1996)
P & C Stadium (1997–   ) at 13208.

Narrow streets (Fayette, Water) a reminder: past was good.
Frank Ferretti rests, but a game awaits!

Take Route 11 to see stars shine ("two teams of nine," Rule 1.01).

So did Chiefs: Jimmy Outlaw (Class of '38)
Hank Sauer ('47)
Bob Keegan ('52)
Willie Horton ('64)

Chiefs have been blessed; Rochester and Buffalo stressed.

Orange pop flows with Hofmann Sausage (born 1879).
No Pepper!
Factory folk enjoy.

All rejoice at Clinton Square. Limited seating available.

Admit one to SkyChiefs.

Baseball @ SoHo, nyc

Arrival on Mercer Street . . . "Ev'rybody off," he shouts.

Coffee fills the air . . . and stomachs, too. Liquor draws a
    crowd. Jazz, liquid, and not cast iron, fuel all.

Poets and wannabes shine.
Lovers dine.
Mightbes whine.

Crime is a rhyme, too.
Grab the bag.
Avoid being tagged.

Fill the eyes on Spring Street. "I" overwhelms "us."

The game? It looks for green, white, and brown. A white ball,
too. It finds Greene Street, galleries, and graffiti, not to
mention "whole food."

The game struggles, limps, and then runs . . .
    from commotion and noise,
        to greener pastures,
          with white lines,
          for "the people,"
        of any means,
        during suntime,
        at any cost,
      between friends,
    near the human heart.

Not here.

Columbus: Summer Game

Columbus, center-laying, is surveyor's dream: land without limit.
        Plat of the town, 1817,
        National road arrives, 1833,
        Broad and High divide.

Not to mention:

Discoverers	Buckeyes
Senators	Solons
Statesmen	Turfs
Bluebirds	Jets
Elite Giants	Colts
Clippers	

Must mention: Opening night, 6/17/32 (Hoover time)

Capitol business stalls.
National pastime calls.

Summer option: some right angles (a grid)
Fall mandate: one rectangle (a gridiron)

Opponents from Louisville are . . .	vile?	No
	evil?	Maybe
	live?	Certainly

Heroes through time:	"Home Run" Breckinridge
	Reb Russell
	Art Shires
	Benny Borgmann
	Sammy Baugh

Please rise and join in the singing . . .

Baseball Along the Genesee

Winds from north fly by;
Rochester folks endure.
Cold Aprils lose to red-hot August sun.

Or white-hot?
Food, for some, balances games.

Names enhance games: "Specs" Toporcer
                        "Comet" Archdeacon
                        Billy "The Kid" Southworth
                        "Slats" McConnell

Faithful come from quadrants,
and South Wedge.

Luke Easter, Grich, Musial.
No weakness there.

Fred "Bone Head" Merkle?
Much laughter there.

1930 boys awesome.
"Specs" owned hurlers.

Strength fails at Silver park,
born during Coolidge-Hoover.

Fans rest at Mt. Hope. "R" on hats means "rest"?
"R" for Rochester!

Wings, take flight on cool air. Preserve shiny image.

Play ball!

Nowhere But Peoria

Central to it all is Peoria—Heartland, Midwest, Breadbasket,
    Midlands, (tallgrass) Prairie, Farmbelt . . .
        where values are tested.

Good or evil? Black and/or white?
Rich v. poor? Mainstream or for a day?

Presidential streets stand out.
Bradley University outstanding.

Chicago? Too far, and busy.
St. Louis? Far, too, but calm.
Indianapolis? Distant, but a cultural cousin.
Roads to the Mississippi show little, except quiet.

Peorians enjoy life on the Illinois River.
(Rails, be gone!)

          ~

The game has been good . . . study old Woodruff.
      . . . is good . . . see (newer) Meinen.
      . . . will be good . . . on warm alluvial soil.

Skies contain (minor) stars with (major) dreams.
Winds from the west blow warm. Pop-ups climb against
some cotton. Softer still is a bunt along third.

          ~

Batter up!

Minor Baseball

The dollar differs. A revocable license easy.

Get programs.
Pencils, too.

Look for "a sphere formed by yarn" (Rule 1.09).

Names? Unknown.
Places? Durham, Davenport, Duluth, and Danville.
Times? Always.

Players play a game of "probable."
Probably not to make it; yes to second, no to bigs.

The chance thrills.
The crowd fills.

To rally once more in Trenton, Tulsa, and Toledo . . .

Perchance to dream? Every day.

Night comes, too.

The road is long, "with many a winding turn."
Little Rock to Midland a long go.
Omaha to Buffalo, too.
Not to mention Tucson to Portland.

Stars have been shining:
        harmon killebrew @ Chattanooga,
        carl yazstrzemski @ Minneapolis,
        jim piersall @ Scranton,
        len tucker @ Peoria.

        Maybe tomorrow.

Home

"The most significant geographical distinction." (1)

"Nurturing shelter." (2)

"The place of inescapable origin and potential and desirable
return." (3)

"A five-sided slab of whitened rubber." (4)

---

(1) J. Douglas Porteous, 1990.
(2) Yi-Fu Tuan, 1975.
(3) Brian Caraher, 1991.
(4) Rule 1.05, 1996.

II.

Some Active
Reconstruction

Memory

" . . . the mental capacity or faculty of retaining and reviving impressions, or of recalling or recognizing previous experiences." *The Random House Dictionary of the English Language,* 1983.

"Memory is central to human life in many different ways. Some of these are purely practical." Fraser Watts, 1995.

"Memory . . . serves to unite individuals, giving them a sense of unity around a common national or ethnic identity." Oliver P. Rafferty, 1995.

"Memory is a complex process, not a simple mental act." James Fentress and Christopher Wickham, 1992.

Section 3, Row H, Seat 5, Doubleday Field, Cooperstown, New York.

"Baseball is cigar smoke, hot-roasted peanuts, *The Sporting News,* winter trades, 'Down in Front,' and the 'Seventh-Inning Stretch.'" Ernie Harwell, 1995.

Game 19, Section 102, Row A, Seat 5, John O'Donnell Stadium, Davenport, Iowa. 52802. May 9, 1994.

At Ten

Distant lights stand.
Dad's grasp entices,
spices an already keen interest.

Close scents stir.
The aroma attracts,
distracts only the idle.

The sphere flies.
The measuring starts;
hearts are moving.

Tallies are counted.
Bases are gained;
strained are looks of foes.

Half-way through?
A rally enthralls,
stalls with double play.

End of seven!
Nervousness is shared;
bared are players' skills.

Nine is all?
Mom says, "Let's go;"
"No," a weak response.

Go home easy.
Day's not the same;
a game again beckons.

July's Game

Grounded balls
topping bladed grass
leave runners stranded
and parched fans. They
show marked thirst.
But peaked (piqued?) interest.

Lifted spheres
through rugged air
stir readied runners
and seasoned fans. They
show wakened faces.
Not failed feelings.

Registered numbers
from journeyed types
excite silenced foes. They
show concerned look.
Not freighted hearts.

End of three; all is well.

Chronology

Hyphened times attract,
    (Sun-day, blue-white skies)
    staging the game for today, for always,
    as white-red spheres fly.

Shortened days detract,
    (September 5)
    condensing the game for this day, for now,
    as time goes by.

Ego-filled days subtract
    (fool's day, clouded skies)
    hurting the game for ever, for all,
    as pride goes by.

Added times need contract,
    (day-night, with power)
    framing the game for the future,
    as rounded sticks apply.

Which days and times prevail? Or must?

Around the Horn

1.

on/enter
First/primary
Hertz
start
Joe Adcock, Milwaukee Braves, 1959
Atlanta Braves, 1995

2.

secondary (vicarious?)
the fiddle
Texas
Bobby Richardson
Chicago White Sox, 1959
Citicorp

3.

tertiary
Al Rosen
avoid 3rd out!
Babe Ruth/"Twinkletoes" Selkirk
Sprint
Brooklyn Dodgers (84-69), 1939

home.
"nurturing shelter" (Tuan, 1975)
"the culmination of the runner's journey" (Garrett, 1976)
finish
"a five-sided slab of whitened rubber" (Rule 1.05)
1600 Marquette Road, Joliet, Illinois 60435
off/exit

Gone But Not . . .

Ollie Carnegie, Buffalo. Steve
Bilko, Detroit. Roberto Clemente.
Comiskey Park (1910-1990).
Griffith, too. Crosley as well.
Gem blades. The Brooklyn Dodgers.
The word "base ball." Joe Engel,
Chattanooga, owner. Pat Pieper, Chicago,
public address. Griesedieck
beer, St. Louis. Frank Ferretti,
Syracuse, fan. Harry Black,
Indianapolis, umpire. Sam DeLeo,
Philadelphia, usher.

May they rest . . .

A Special Care

Soaring in the heart is a feeling now enjoyed
  of glee,
  of pride,
  of owning,
  of many things, not removable,

For me, the person/the player,
  the one who writes, writes again, and caresses

Things precious . . . and sacred?

Yes, and a treasure to keep
  and to love . . . fervently,
    intensely, ·
    daily.

Musts now seem feeble; no block stands.

The list (first, second, third) is small.
  Home is cherished.

No one steals or takes . . . or changes, either.

The game and the words are of me and, in part, of you . . .
  and will be so.

  For now and for ever.

    What else might there be?

A Fevered Time

Clouds of war obscure the game.
Worshipping fans flood Ebbets.
Enter Monte Irvin? No.

Enter Jackie (Roosevelt Robinson).

Talent shines amid white fans.
His position? Second base.
His race, too . . . but Jackie wins.

Some bases have been stolen.
But a respect has been earned.
Some complain . . . but Jackie wins.

Black cats and taunts do their thing.
Brooklyn victories add up.
Insults come . . . but Jackie wins.

Fans see double (black and white).
Jackie sees too much, of course.
Mates look down . . . but Jackie wins.

Numbers bear out basic skills.
Hits outweigh errors for sure.
Some look askance . . . but Jackie wins.

Today Jackie is at rest.
A peace and some grace prevail.
Skills outran hues . . . and Jackie won.

A new day dawns for the game.
Balls, bats and games still await.

Does some understanding come?

Second

One stands between one and two—
the sun shines.

Move the dirt below the feet—
the sun blinds.

Edge to right; lean to left now—
the "fwack" tells.

Talk soon to short; read the pitch—
must see well.

Try to leap high; heave to first—
turn left fast.

Front must move with back to plate—
legs must last.

A setting sun is plenty—
tough to squeeze.

One final out to get now—
more games, please.

Aches and Pains

Lucious Benjamin Appling
shortstop
born April 2, 1907
batted .388, 1936
died January 3, 1991
aged 83 years, 9 months, 1 day

Sweet be thy rest

Safe?

1a.
20 lb. 25% cotton fibre
an instrument for writing
a focus
(delicious) diction
a grammar well crafted
images, themes, symbols:
insight;
word processing?

what else matters?

1b.
blue sky
a 90-foot square and a sphere formed by yarn
a plan
moving 'em along
a three-run homer
"hold 'em and go home"
a time-free treasure;
writing our lives?

what else matters?

Down in the Count

Dyads reign: rich and poor/
        have and have not/
           high and low/
              (down and out?)

No questions surround the anthem/
        no admittance for the lowly/
          no luck theirs/

Numeric pleasures lacking:
        one cold one/
          double to left/
            triple to gap/
              four bagger/
                five-run sixth?

Double play: no job, no coins/
        sacrifice: every day/
          walk: constantly/
            victories: none/

Stop signs (////) aplenty/

1890/one eight nine zero

figures tell the tale:
>Detroit: 205,000 people. Colorado: 412,198.
>Mormon "Manifesto": no more plural marriages.
>62,947,714 folks in USA, 11.9% Negro.
>Illiteracy: 13.3%.
>Dixie: 48 cities of more than 10,000!

names on bill of sale:
>Wounded Knee Creek, South Dakota,
>Brooklyn vs. Louisville, World Series,
>"The White House at Night," Vincent van Gogh,
>John Boyle O'Reilly, defender of Jews, Blacks, Indians,
>Frederick Jackson Turner: "frontier closed,"
>Asa Yoelson, age 4 (later Al Jolson),
>Separate Car Act, Louisiana,
>Chicago Cubs, West Side Park,
>Sherman Antitrust Act,
>Isaac Murphy, (Negro) jockey, Derby winner abaord "Riley."

for sale:
        Coca-Cola,
        Remington type-writers,
        American Tobacco Company,
        Steinway pianos,
        Pabst Blue Ribbon (age 46).

beyond the veil:
        James A. Garfield,
        JeffersonDavis,
        Emily Dickinson.

those were the days!

Scores and Tallies

Rule 10.03

How to Prove a Box Score

(c) A box score is in balance (or proved) when the total of the team's times at bat, bases on balls received, hit batters, sacrifice bunts, sacrifice flies and batters awarded first base because of interference or obstruction equals the total of that team's runs, players left on base and the opposing team's put-outs.

How to "Prove" a Life

(d) A life is in balance (or proved) when, ironically, the quantity and quality of charitable acts directed toward others is judged to be sufficient by a higher power, not found on a baseball diamond or in a pressbox. Counting the exact number of such acts of charity is not necessary. An awareness of the need to sacrifice daily is essential, however.

Landscape: Baseball

Driven spheres
In the sky chart centerbound routes,
Saying nothing

Over second.
Players crane necks
        skyward

In center's
Direction. Blue skies only
Show summer

Waiting to be enjoyed
By one/all. You

Turn from the game.
Nights swallows all
In sight.
In the distance lights well burning.

Fans go, and their joy-filled smiling.

(Gervase Toelle [1921-1967]: "Landscape: Niagara," 1961)

Babe Ruth, Our Hero

a Baltimore birth;
baby had girth;
what's the worry?

shirts to make?
pitches to take!
rbi's in a flurry.

Boston to New York;
pass the knife and fork;
the high life in a surrey!

books can wait;
baseball the fate;
America the richer.

a drink to take;
an appointment to make;
kids get the picture.

a bond to Claire;
a marriage in thin air;
love moves quicker.

homers aplenty;
walks were many;
fun for all.

in '48 dying;
America was crying;
a legend falls.

Aaron/Maris give chase;
they recall Babe's face;
he still stands tall.

forget now the hours;
the man still towers;
the Babe was ours!

Artificial Class

green
multi-purpose
hotter,
"like the Astrodome stuff."

blotchy
patchy
slick,
"like the Pittsburgh and St. Louis stuff."

inexpensive
tough
removable,
"like the Cincinnati stuff."

true hops
straight lines
more hits,
"like the Seattle stuff."

fewer errors
faster cleanup
better drainage,
"like the Philadelphia and Montreal stuff."

"I, too, dislike it."

Seven Year Old's Dream

dry pants

a full tummy

mom

a cold soda/pop

Box 14 Row F Seat 5
Rosenblatt Stadium
Omaha, Nebraska

ice cream

74 degrees

Baseball, 1845-

Whose labels could be better? Abner, Stan, Dummy, Nellie, Hoyt.
Much delight there.

Slow change these days: Jose, Julio, Barry, George.
Great names last: Gehrig, Mays, Feller, Paige, Cobb.

Numbers flourish.
They enhance: Ted's .406 and Roger's 61.
They numb: crowd of 19,257 at Cincinnati on 4-14-08.
They play a part:

9	innings
3	outs
0	pepper games
9	players
0	clocks

9-30-90 (end of old Comiskey).
Rates and fractions, dollars and percents find blue sky.

So does dreaming. Soft wind. White lines. Flag unfurled. Two dogs
with the works. Stress-free for now. Many stitches of red cotton.

History?

     Providence Clams   Alexander Cartwright

         Chattanooga Lookouts   Clyde Kluttz

             Pittsburgh Crawfords   Warren Spahn

           Durham Bulls

Science lives, too. A pleasant geometry.

     Given: worries divided by baseball equals fun.

Error	Pete Rose	Home Run	Babe Ruth
Caught Stealing	Joe Jackson	Stolen Base	Brooklyn to LA
Sacrifice	Roberto Clemente	K	Sandy Koufax
Wild Pitch	Ryne Duren	Triple	Duke, Willie, Mick

Pitching wins games. Throw strikes.

Avoid the strike zone. Vary the avoidance, we're told.

               Grab the ball? It grabs you.

                  Batter up!

Some Musings on Ice

[The view differs-
        one sees no problem,
        the other does.

Summer comes: long days, desked life,
in a "Court" or "Circle." The cold is no foe; it cools the drink.
The feeling frees us. Bottoms up!]

        "That's the end of 1st inning, fans."

[Winter comes: short days, forged life,
in "Apt 2." The cold frightens; it freezes, hurts the pipes and
the feet/hands. Why can't it be summer?]

        "We'll be right back after these words."

[Winter comes, but the crackle doesn't annoy. Nor does the cost. Add cardigan. Who needs a thaw? Not the well-to-do. Here's to ya!]

> "It's time, ladies and gentlemen, for the 7th inning stretch."

[Summer comes, but no cool/rest is given. The blocks are not affordable. The cubes aren't, either. Peel the threads now. Why can't it be winter?]

> "Please drive safely, everyone."

Nostalgia

"A desire to return in thought or in fact to a former time in one's life, to one's home, or to one's family and friends." *The Random House Dictionary of the English Language*, 1983.

"... the tendency to contrast an idealized Past, when families were presumably strong, stable, and caring, with a decadent, fallen Present." Arlene Skolnick, 1991.

"Nostalgia makes presence, theatrically, but convincingly, for it represents the thing or person or place we care for as an oasis of presence in a desert of loss. It is this juxtaposition of the negative with the positive, this enveloping of the negative, of change, of disappearance, of our having lost touch, of our having diminished, which seems to isolate the good for us and momentarily stop time." Ralph Harper, 1985.

August 10, 1992, 7:05pm: Ramp 4, Section C, Row E, Seat 001, Silver Stadium, 500 Norton Street, Rochester, New York. 14621.

Ted Williams, 1941.

Pittsburgh Pirates, 1960.

Toledo Mud Hens, 1974.

III.
Indoor Games

Definition

Nubber, noun. 1. a ball weakly hit on the ground off the very end of the bat to the opposite side of the infield that the batter is facing. The motion of the ball upon leaving the bat is clockwise off the right-handed batter's bat (rolling toward second or first) but counterclockwise off the left-handed batter's bat (rolling toward third base or shortstop). 2. one who nubs?

One Revocable License, Please

Warm winds satisfy.
Clouds disappoint.
Rounded bats attract.
Ball, too.
Listen for "fwack."

Event Code: Baseball.

Admit one, and admit me, subject to conditions.
Good this day only? For today and for ever. All ways and always.
Price? Invaluable (tax included).

No refunds?	Fine
No exchange?	Good
No pass-outs?	OK

Seat 5 (22" across)

Section 10   Aisle 2

rain check information: retain
possession of this rain check
until the game for which this
ticket admits holder has been
played. Should such game not
constitute a regulation game
under official baseball rule
4.10(c), this rain check may
be exchanged for the date this
game is re-scheduled this year.
This ticket is not refundable.

Warning

The ticket holder assumes all risk and danger incidental to the game of Baseball whether occuring prior to, during, or subsequent to the actual playing of the game, including specifically (but not exclusively) the joys of being positively impacted by the interaction of baseballs, bats, soft drinks, and peanuts, and agrees that the participating clubs, their agents, and players and other individuals are certainly liable for the fun resulting from such wonderful causes.

Theories, Very Possible   38

Unique theory. Must sell. Links the fallacy of composition with the meaning(s) of baseball. Explains how the amount of career triples recorded by Nelson Fox (112) relates to the game's elasticity. Winner at 1991 Harrisburg IdeaMart. PC all the way. Real collector's item. A cutting edge issue. Fax resume. Call Lester at 831-2426.

Religion and the Game

All rise and sing.
Warm winds comfort.

Two teams of nine (not seven-sided) strive.

E-6? Lord, Have Mercy!
Sins/errors a basic style.

Questions arise:

Gospel? To follow other steps (like Ruth, Mays, Mantle).
Rally time? A resurrection: soon (and very soon!).
Two-run homer? It would have been enough.
Pitching? An amazing grace.
Preaching? It wins the day.
Salvation? Essential, though "not your own doing."
Grace? It is for giving.

Solution follows:

Hope, like hurling, anchors all.

Collect memories: Ruth, Aaron, Bonds. Marvelous fellows(hip).
: 1969 Chicago White Sox? Pardon their offense.
: "Ping" Bodie, catcher. May he rest . . .

Collect coins, too.

(Another) batter up! Vespers soon.
It should be with luck!

No pepper. No hubris, either.

The Game and Time

Major shift: time for . . . and time for . . .
                 give way to time-less baseball.

Warm winds and coin carry fans quickly.
Sun time better than night time.
Little worry.

A large pleasure awaits. Unfortunate few "do time."

The game evolves: .245 average for league
in 1893 (Harrison-Cleveland time).

Things get better in "railroad time." No more three noons.

Anthem brings a smile.

No hurry, but frames change.

Ballspeed to home? 90 mph (the going rate).
Steal of third? No seconds told.

Time changes: Seiko now at Yankees.

Times change, but good ones last.
Gehrig, Williams, Mays, and Koufax.

Successive instants are measured, analog and digital:
Longines at Shibe,
Bulova at Ebbets,
Elgin at old Comiskey.

Final frame? Clock-free memory of the games and game.

Next time? A dream away!

Still and again the enjoyment comes.

Riddle

I en-square and designate;
play becomes ruled thereby:
left or right,
right or wrong.
Play ball!

The Chart

Oxygen
O
15.999

Aluminum
Al
26.982

Helium
He
4.0026

Hydrogen
H
1.0079

Nylon
216 stitches
U.S. $11.50
Can. $14.50

Neon
N
20.180

Silicon
Si
28.086

Lead
Pb
207.2

Iron
Fe
55.847

Music and the Game

Four flats and 3/4 time bring the anthem. Pride, too.
No heed for past places "where the field was warm and green."

Take good notes.
Read between the lines.

Rock the pitcher and his staff. Look for "bent pitches."
No rests.

Ragged play makes for rag(ged) time, "white music played black."

The blues, "every happening an inconvenience," follow.
Foes are "looking up at down."

Swing. Bunt. Hit. Run. Score. Count.
One-syllable fun there.

Key of D in 3/4 time: "Take Me Out." Sing moderately.
Use improvisation. Resist composition.

Bottom of 9th? Sharp single up middle (mid-range?) wins it.

Gospel for some: the game is the way, truth, and life.

Critics agree.   There is expressive purpose, purity of tone,
                  propulsive rhythm, sinuous lines.

                          Let's play two.

Limited Power

allgame Tonig t
7:3 pm
Arkan as v. Shrevepo t

Ordeal

noun. 1. A difficult or painful experience, especially one that severely tests character or endurance. See Synonyms at "trial." *American Heritage Dictionary of the English Language*, 3rd edition, 1992.

2. E.g., throwing the baseball plateward against Ted Williams, 1941.

3. E.g., appearing in the batter's box against Sandy Koufax, 1963.

Manager's Guide

When ahead by:	When behind by:
1 bunt	1 steal second
2 sacrifice	2 hit and run
3 swing away	3 swing away
4 hope	4 pray
5 pray	5 hope
6 smile	6 try to smile
7 congratulate	7 console
8 thank God	8 don't blame
9 don't argue	9 pray for rain
10 deflect the credit	10 pray for more rain

Clip and Save

Numbers and the Game

Four flats and 3/4 time bring anthem. Pride, too.

Forever, and with joy, the sums arrive:
    1 ball to throw home
    2 strikes, then caution
    3 Ruth, Babe

Given: worries divided by baseball equals fun.[1]
    4 wide ones earn first
    5 Bench
    6 outs per frame

    3-2-3 hard way double play
    7 thinning stretch
    8 Stargell
    9 innings to count[2]

Great numbers:	4,256 (Rose hits)
Pretty numbers:	48,041 (Baltimore seats)
Historic numbers:	6-28-70 (last day at Forbes, Pittsburgh)
Sad numbers:	721 F. Supp. 906, 924 [S. D. Ohio 1989]
	(*Rose v. Giamatti*)

Games beat gaming: Bobby Thomson (10-3-51) conquers Pick 4.
Digits and fractions: Maris (1961/61/162) beats Daily 3.

Prime numbers: 3 (Ruth), 7 (Mantle), and 29 (Carew).

Just the facts: Yankees and White Sox brawl on 6-13-57.
Now the fax: 312-451-5116 for White Sox today.

New math: 42,633 had one great time vs. Yanks in Kansas City in 1980.[3]

Metric: 51,723 moved happy feet, not meters, to Negro League game in Chicago in 1943.

Count me in! Other innumerates, too.
Admit one. And admit me!

---

[1]forever

[2]subject to change

[3]a record

Baseball and the Law

Whereas baseball was and is intended for the enjoyment
      of all and,
Whereas Willie Mays thrilled millions with incontrovertible
      skills and,
Whereas runs and rallies render boredom "void on its face,"
Be it resolved that baseball will never be devitalized.

Articles of Agreement:

3 strikes	9 frames
3 outs	0 clocks
2 teams	1 affirmative decision
0 pepper	

Argue the truth? Argue the evidence!
The evidence: thousands attend per game from Boston to LA.
The experience: warm wind, a white sphere, a rounded bat.

500-foot homers?	dubious
Babies in mezzanine?	dormant
Fan dissatisfaction?	inadmissible

In the World Series, Bronx, New York

<u>In Re</u> the Game of Baseball:

Tony Kubek, ss	}	
Bobby Richardson, 2b	}	
Tom Tresh, of	}	
Mickey Mantle, of	}	
Roger Maris, of	}	October 2, 1963
et al.	}	
-vs-	}	
Sandy Koufax, p	}	

the people having heard the evidence and testimony of the parties (duly sworn and examined in open Stadium); and considering all the evidence and being fully advised in the premises,

FIND AS FOLLOWS:

1. that the American people are now, and have been for more than 140 years, lovers of the game of baseball.

Batter up, and hold us all harmless!

witnesseth:

Food and the Game

Menu   Price

frozen ropes
pickles, served at hot corner
cans of corn
Sno-Cones in center
rhubarb
chili (in April)
donuts
lollipop curves
rolls (to the infield)
Cracker Jack (born 1893) $2.25
McRuns, McHits, McErrors
hot dogs
beef (with umpires)
onions (turn clockwise)

No pepper   No smoking

Direct your attention to home plate; save your dough.

Use Rolaids (from Warner-Lambert).
Tums, too.

No preservatives, just great tradition.

Think before you drink!

Batter up!

Villanelle

There comes a time to tip the cap,
as players strive to win the game.
Watch the ball now; who has the bat?

The ball thrown home flies toward the man.
The pitcher waits; the batter tame?
There comes a time to tip the cap.

Bat and arms move. He swings so late . . .
the ball zooms foul; the count's the same.
Watch the ball now; who has the bat?

New spheres to throw; "Who's the man?"
Not the catcher, Johnson by name.
There comes a time to tip the cap.

Innings now pass; who hits the mat?
The home team sure. It takes the game.
Watch the ball now; who has the bat?

Day's now done. Put on the hats.
Home proceeding, we mention names.
There comes a time to tip the cap.
Watch the ball now; who has the bat?

The Corporate Game

Time fades on arrival.
Numbers swirl at the sound of "fwack."
Follow "revocable license" as anthem sings.
Pose, too, using Kodak. Save the negative. Enjoy the positive.

recognize: the green of John Deere, on dirt.
read: Rawlings, Sony, Budweiser, Louisville Slugger.
report home: "everybody safe," MCI.
rally: might comes from Wheaties of General Mills.

eat?   dogs from Oscar Mayer (not Bill Meyer, '52 Pirates boss)
       treats from Cracker Jack (born 1893 from Borden)
       pizza from the Hut (1958 start)
       no pepper (from McCormick, born 1889, Baltimore)

relief?   ATMs. All That Matters   .
          MACs. Money Always Counts
          Rolaids, too, from Warner-Lambert

relax!   seats: American Seating, Grand Rapids
liquids: Coca-Cola, Atlanta
popcorn: Beatrice, Chicago

thinning stretch: Kohler parts and Ft. Howard towels

end of nine? Bring in Brinks (born 1859, Buchanan time)

Exit to Street

Another time . . .

B4Real

You know, like, baseball is, like, OK, but, you know, it's not, like, a happenin' thing. I mean, for sure, there's only one ball, and, like, everybody's throwing it around. I don't know. At times the pitcher just stands there. I mean really. He's sour. Is there another game tomorrow? One, like, I mean, this one I'm watching? Will it be a bomb or will it be, like, lame?

Anagram

Q. Baseball's Total Package?

A. Mail us . . . Musial!

Additional Reading

Altherr, Thomas L. "A Swing and a Myth: The Persistence of Baseball in the American Imagination." *Cooperstown Symposium on Baseball and the American Culture (1989)*. Alvin L. Hall, ed. Westport, CT: Meckler in association with the State University of New York College at Oneonta, 1991: 60–72.

Anderson, Dave. "In October, Baseball Is the Best." *New York Times*, October 20, 1996, late ed., sec. 8, p. 1.

Behm, Richard. "Looking for the Baseball." *The Southern Review*. vol. 32, no. 1 (Winter 1996): 2–6.

Biemiller, Lawrence. "Baseball the Soul of America? Sit in the Sun for a Doubleheader. You'll See." *The Chronicle of Higher Education* (May 4, 1994): A 55.

Bjarkman, Peter C. *Baseball & the Game of Life: Stories for the Thinking Fans*. Otisville, NY: Birch Book Press, 1990.

Blaisdell, Lowell D. "Legends as an Expression of Baseball Memory." *Journal of Sport History*, vol. 19, no. 3 (Winter 1992): 227–243.

Blake, Mike. *Baseball Chronicles: An Oral History of Baseball Through the Decades*. Cincinnati: Betterway Books, 1994.

Bodnar, Stephen. "Prehistoric Baseball." *Elysian Fields Quarterly*, vol. 12, no. 1 (Hot Stove League Issue 1993): 73.

Boswell, Thomas. *How Life Imitates the World Series: An Inquiry Into the Game*. Garden City, NY: Doubleday, 1982.

Bowering, George Henry. *Poem and Other Baseballs*. Coatsworth, ON: Black Moss Press, 1976.

———. "Baseball, a Poem in the Magic Number 9." In *The Grand-Slam Book of Canadian Writing*. John Bell, ed. Porters Lake, NS: Pottersfield Press, 1993: 60–62.

Braggs, Earl S. "The Baseball Boys of 1964." *African American Review*, vol. 28, no. 4 (Winter 1994): 585–587.

Brennan, Matthew C. "The Transparent Baseball: 'Making Contact' As Visionary Experience." *NINE: A Journal of Baseball History and Social Policy Perspectives*. vol. 6, no. 1 (Fall 1997): 93–100.

Briley, Ronald. "Baseball and American Cultural Values." *Magazine of History*, vol. 7, no. 1 (Summer 1992): 61–63.

Broeg, Bob, and William J. Miller, Jr. *Baseball From a Different Angle*. South Bend, IN: Diamond Communications, 1988.

Brosnan, Jim. "The Fantasy World of Baseball." *Atlantic Monthly*, vol. 213, no. 4 (April 1964): 69–72.

Brown, Bill. "The Meaning of Baseball in 1992 (with Notes on the Post-American)." *Public Culture*, vol. 4, no. 1 (Fall 1991): 43–69.

Buchwald, Emilie, and Ruth Roston, eds. *This Sporting Life.* Minneapolis: Milkweed Editions, 1987.

Candelaria, Cordelia. *Seeking the Perfect Game: Baseball in American Literature.* New York: Greenwood Press, 1989.

Caraher, Brian G. "The Poetics of Baseball: An American Domestication of the Mathematically Sublime." *American Studies*, vol. 32, no. 1 (Spring 1991): 85–100.

Carney, Gene. *Romancing the Horsehide: Baseball Poems on Players and the Game.* Jefferson, NC: McFarland, 1993.

Cataneo, David. *Peanuts and Crackerjack: A Treasury of Baseball Legends and Lore.* Nashville: Rutledge Hill Press, 1991.

Catton, Bruce. "The Great American Game." *American Heritage,* vol. 10, no. 3 (April 1959): 16–25, 86.

Clark, Tom. *Fan Poems.* Plainfield, VT: North Atlantic Books, 1976.

Clarke, Alden. "O Ebbets Field." *Sports Illustrated*, vol. 12, no. 10 (March 7, 1960): 31.

Coffin, Tristram Potter. *The Old Ball Game: Baseball in Folklore and Fiction.* New York: Herder and Herder, 1971.

Cohen, Marvin. *Baseball the Beautiful: Decoding the Diamond.* New York: Links Press, 1974.

Cohen, Ted. "There Are No Ties at First Base." *Yale Review*, vol. 79, no. 2 (Winter 1990): 314–322.

Conquergood, Dwight. "Poetics, Play, Process, and Power: The Performative Turn in Anthropology." *Text and Performance Quarterly*, vol. 9, no. 1 (January 1989): 82–88.

Crepeau, Richard . "Urban and Rural Images in Baseball." *Journal of Popular Culture,* vol. 9, no. 2 (Fall 1975): 315–324.

Dillard, Annie. "We Already Know You Like Baseball." In *Mornings Like This: Found Poems.* New York: HarperCollins, 1995: 49.

Dodge, Tom. *A Literature of Sports.* Lexington, MA: D.C. Heath and Company, 1980.

Downes, Terrence B. *When Winter Takes a Stroll: Reflections on Life and Baseball.* Harwich, MA: Terrence B. Downes, 1996.

Evans, David. "Poetry and Sport." *Arete: The Journal of Sport Literature,* vol. 4, no. 2 (Spring 1987): 141–145.

Farrell, James T. "Baseball: A Fan's Notes." *American Scholar,* vol. 48 (Summer 1979): 391–394.

Fehler, Gene. *Center Field Grasses: Poems from Baseball.* Jefferson, NC: McFarland, 1991.

———. *I Hit the Ball! Baseball Poems for the Young.* Jefferson, NC: McFarland, 1996.

Frank, Lawrence. *Playing Hardball: The Dynamics of Baseball Folk Speech.* New York: Peter Lang, 1983.

Garrett, Roland. "The Metaphysics of Baseball." *Philosophy Today,* (Fall 1976): 209–226.

Giamatti, A. Bartlett. *Take Time for Paradise: Americans and Their Games.* New York: Summit Books, 1989.

———. "Baseball and the American Character," *Harper's Magazine,* vol. 273, no. 1637 (October 1986): 27, 30.

Gmelch, George J. "Baseball Magic." *Trans-ACTION,* vol. 8, no. 8 (June 1971): 39–41, 54.

Gould, Stephen Jay. "The Creation Myths of Cooperstown: Or Why the Cardiff Giants are an Unbeatable and Inappropriately Named Team." *Natural History,* vol. 98 (November 1989): 14–24.

Grella, George. "Baseball and the American Dream." *Massachusetts Review,* vol. 16, no. 3 (Summer 1975): 550–567.

Griffin, Walter. "Sliding Home." *America,* vol. 159, no. 10 (October 15, 1988): 247.

Halberstam, David. "Baseball and the National Mythology." *Harper's Magazine,* vol. 241, no. 1444 (September 1970): 22–25.

Hall, Donald. *Fathers Playing Catch With Sons.* San Francisco: North Point Press, 1985.

Harper, Michael S. "No. 24." In *Nightmare Begins Responsibility.* Urbana: University of Illinois Press, 1975: 92–93.

Harrison, Robert L. *Green Fields and White Lines: Baseball Poems.* Jefferson, NC: McFarland & Company, Inc., Publishers, 1995.

Healy, Dave, and Paul Healy. "Half-Cultivated Fields: The Symbolic Landscapes of Baseball." *Minneapolis Review of Baseball,* vol. 8 (Fall 1989): 31–37, 64.

Heyen, William. "The Stadium." In *Depth of Field.* Baton Rouge: LSU Press, 1970: 51.

Higgs, Robert J. *Laurel & Thorn: The Athlete in American Literature.* Lexington: University Press of Kentucky, 1980.

Hildebidle, John. "The Intellectual Game: Baseball and the Life of the Mind," *The New England Review and Bread Loaf Quarterly,* vol. 7, no. 2 (Winter 1984): 252–264.

Holden, Jonathan. "Poetry, Baseball: The Pleasures of the Text." *Antaeus,* no. 59 (Autumn 1987): 115–126.

———. "How to Play Night Baseball." In *Design for a House.* Columbia, MO: University of Missouri Press, 1972: 36.

Hopkins, Lee Bennett. *Extra Innings: Baseball Poems.* San Diego: Harcourt Brace Jovanovich, Publishers, 1993.

Huizinga, Johan. *Homo Ludens: A Study of the Play-Element in Culture.* Tr. R.F.C. Hull. London: Routledge & K. Paul, 1980.

Johnson, Don, ed. *Hummers, Knucklers, and Slow Curves: Contemporary Baseball Poems.* Urbana: University of Illinois Press, 1991.

Jolliff, William. "The Theologian Talks Baseball." *Christian Century,* vol. 110, no. 11 (April 7, 1993): 374.

Kagan, Donald. "George Will's Baseball-A Conservative Critique." *Public Interest,* no. 101 (Fall 1990): 3–20.

Kanfer, Stefan. "The Greatest Game." *Time,* vol. 101 (April 30 1973): 82.

Katovich, Mike A. "Humor in Baseball: Functions and Dysfunctions," *Journal of American Culture,* vol. 16, no. 2 (Summer 1993): 7–15.

Klinkowitz, Jerry, ed. *Writing Baseball.* Urbana: University of Illinois Press, 1991.

Knudson, R.R. and May Swenson, eds/comps. *American Sports Poems.* New York: Orchard Books, 1988.

Lefkowitz, Mary R. "The Poet as Athlete," *Journal of Sport History,* vol. 11, no. 2 (Summer 1984): 18–24.

Leitner, Irving A. *Baseball: Diamond in the Rough.* New York: Abelard-Schuman, 1972.

Malarcher, David. "Oscar Charleston." On *Diamond Cuts: A Compilation of Baseball Songs and Poetry* (compact disc HFM 003), Jeff Campbell, comp. Washington, DC: Hungry for Music, 1997.

Mayer, Robert. *Baseball and Men's Lives: The True Confessions of a Skinny-Marink.* New York: Bantam Doubleday Dell Publishing Group, Inc., 1994.

McDowell, Robert. "When Baseball Made Out." *The Hudson Review,* vol. 48, no. 3 (Autumn 1995): 411–424.

Meissner, Bill. "Something About Certain Old Baseball Fields." *Midwest Quarterly*, vol. 36, no. 4 (Summer 1995): 406–407.

Memmott, A. James. "Wordsworth in the Bleachers: The Baseball Essays of Roger Angell." *Journal of American Culture*, vol. 5, no. 4 (Winter 1982): 52–56.

Moore, Jim. *Ernest Thayer's 'Casey at the Bat': Background and Characters of Baseball's Most Famous Poem*. Jefferson, NC: McFarland & Co., 1994.

Moore, Marianne. "Baseball and Writing." In *The Collected Poems*. New York: Macmillan and Company, 1968: 221–223.

Morison, Elting E. "Positively the Last Word on Baseball." *American Heritage*, vol. 37, no. 5 (August-September 1986): 83–89.

Morrison, Lillian, comp. *At the Crack of the Bat: Baseball Poems*. New York: Hyperion Books for Children, 1992.

———. *Sprints and Distances: Sports in Poetry and the Poetry in Sport*. New York: Thomas Y. Crowell, 1965.

Mosher, Stephen. "Fielding Our Dreams: Rounding Third in Dyersville." *Sociology of Sport Journal*, vol. 8, no. 3 (September 1991): 272–280.

Muise, Louise A. "Ode to/To a First Baseman." *English Journal*, vol. 77, no. 3 (March 1988): 88.

Nauen, Elinor, ed. *Diamonds Are a Girl's Best Friend: Women Writers on Baseball*. Boston: Faber and Faber, 1994.

Neelon, Ann. "World Series." *The Gettysburg Review,* vol. 5, no. 3 (Summer 1992): 460–461.

Newcomb, John Timberman. "'Say It Ain't Snow, Joe': On the White Mythology of American Baseball." *South Atlantic Quarterly,* vol. 85, no. 3 (Summer 1986): 297–300.

Oles, Carole. "The Interpretation of Baseball." *Poetry,* vol. 152, no. 3 (June 1988): 133.

Oriard, Michael. *Sporting With the Gods: The Rhetoric of Play and Game in American Culture.* New York: Cambridge University Press, 1991.

Orodenker, Richard. *The Writers' Game: Baseball Writing in America.* New York: Twayne Publishers, 1996.

Palmatier, Robert A. *Sports Talk: A Dictionary of Sports Metaphors.* New York: Greenwood Press, 1989.

Parker, Ev. "Ode to Casey Stengel." *The National Pastime: A Review of Baseball History,* vol. 14 (1994): 112.

Plimpton, George, ed. *The Norton Book of Sports.* New York: W. W. Norton & Company, 1992.

Porter, Dennis. "The Perilous Quest: Baseball as Folk Drama." *Critical Inquiry,* vol. 4, no. 1 (Autumn 1977) 143–157.

Roberts, Terence J. "Sport and Strong Poetry." *Journal of the Philosophy of Sport,* vol. 22, nos. 3-4 (1995): 94–107.

Rogoff, Jay. *The Cutoff.* Washington, DC: Word Works, 1995.

Ross, Murray. "Football Red and Baseball Green: The Heroics and Bucolics of American Sport." *Chicago Review*, vol. 22, nos. 2 and 3 (January-February 1971): 30–40.

Ruscoe, Michael. *Baseball: A Treasury of Art and Literature.* New York: Macmillan Publishing Co., 1993.

Samuels, V. "Baseball Slang." *American Speech*, vol. 2, no. 5 (February 1927): 255–256.

Schacht, Mike. *Mudville Diaries: A Book of Baseball Memories.* New York: Avon Books, 1996.

Shannon, Mike. *The Writers' Game.* South Bend, IN: Diamond Communications, 1992.

———. "The Art of Baseball Poetry." In *The Day Satchell Paige and the Pittsburgh Crawfords Came to Hertford, NC: Baseball Stories and Poems.* Jefferson, NC: McFarland & Co., 1992: 98.

Sheed, Wilfrid. "Why Sports Matter." *Wilson Quarterly*, vol. 19, no. 1 (Winter 1995): 11–25.

Solomon, Eric. "Earl Wasserman, Johns Hopkins, Baseball and Me." *Johns Hopkins Magazine*, vol. 35, no. 2 (April 1984): 10, 12–16.

———. "The Boys of Summer Grow Older: Roger Kahn and the Baseball Memoir." *Baseball History*, vol. 2 (Summer 1987): 27–46.

Spencer, Kathleen Walsh. "Dreamflight to Cedar Rapids." *Fan: A Baseball Magazine*, no. 24 (Fall/Winter 1996): 41.

Stone, Ira F. "Well, It's a Game, No? A Meditation on Poetry and Baseball." *SABR Review of Books*, vol. 2 (1987): 64–70.

Swenson, May. "Analysis of Baseball." In *More Poems to Solve* (New York: Charles Scribner's Sons, 1971): 39.

Thorn, John. *Baseball: Our Game.* New York: Penguin Books, 1995.

Torreson, Rodney. *The Ripening of Pinstripes.* Brownsville, OR: Story Line Press, 1998.

Trujillo, Nick, and Bob Krizek. "Emotionality in the Stands and in the Field: Expressing Self Through Baseball." *Journal of Sport & Social Issues,* vol. 18, no. 4 (November 1994): 303–325.

Vanderwerken, David L., and Spencer K. Wertz, eds. *Sport Inside Out: Readings in Literature and Philosophy.* Ft. Worth, TX: Texas Christian University Press, 1985.

Vogt, Del C. *Baseball History in Limerick Verse & in Sketch.* Milwaukee: Greenfield House, 1981.

Voigt, David Q. "Reflections on Diamonds: American Baseball and American Culture." *Journal of Sport History,* vol. 1, no. 1 (Spring 1974): 3–25.

Wallace, Joseph, ed. *The Baseball Anthology: 125 Years of Stories, Poems, Articles, Photographs, Drawings, Interviews, Cartoons, and Other Memorabilia.* New York: Abrams, 1994.

Weigel, George. "Politically-Correct Baseball." *Commentary*, vol. 98, no. 5 (November 1994): 46–51.

Westbrook, Deeanne. *Ground Rules: Baseball and Myth*. Champaign: University of Illinois Press, 1996.

Whelpley, Rodd. "Going to a New Ballpark." *Elysian Fields Quarterly*, vol. 11, no. 4 (World Series Issue 1992): 6.

Wiles, Tim. "Who's on Verse? Baseball Fans are Poets, and Poets are Fans." *New York Times*, March 31, 1996, late ed., sec. 8: 13.

Will, George. *Men at Work: The Craft of Baseball*. New York: Macmillan, 1990.

Williams, Peter. "Thirties Eclogue." *Spitball: the Literary Baseball Magazine*, vol. 47 (Summer 1994): 32.

Wimmer, Dick. *Baseball Fathers, Baseball Sons*. New York: Morrow, 1988.

Wormser, Baron. "Listening To a Baseball Game." *Paris Review*, vol. 32, no. 115 (Summer 1990): 200–202.

About the Author

Edward R. Ward lives in Bogota, New Jersey. He was born in Joliet, Illinois and raised on the Chicago White Sox.